A Sister, a Poet,
A Spiritual Spoken Word

A Sister, a Poet,
A Spiritual Spoken Word

Trina Brigham

THE REGENCY
PUBLISHERS

Copyright © 2022 Trina Brigham.

All rights reserved. No part of this publication may be reproduced, distributed, or transmitted in any form or by any electronic or mechanical means, including information storage and retrieval systems, without a prior written permission from the publisher, except by reviewers, who may quote brief passages in a review, and certain other noncommercial uses permitted by the copyright law.

ISBN: 978-1-958517-30-7   (Paperback Edition)
ISBN: 978-1-958517-31-4   (Hardcover Edition)
ISBN: 978-1-958517-29-1   (E-book Edition)

Book Ordering Information

The Regency Publishers, International
7 Bell Yard London WO2A2JR

info@theregencypublishers.com
www.theregencypublishers.international
+44 20 8133 0466

Printed in the United States of America

Dedications

To my heavenly father the almighty creator Thank you for blessing me to carry out your mandate. You've given me powerful words of life to speak into the hearts of your people in such a time as this. Words of truth, hope and inspiration is very much needed in these perilous times.

In memory of
Irene and Willie Lee Brigham,

I salute you for your inspiration and encouragement.

I'm thankful for the love and support you have always shown me throughout the years. I'm honored and blessed by the Most-high to have been loved by such beautiful parents. Until we meet again, R.I.P. Love your baby girl.

Thanks family

Tina Davis, Willie Brigham, Tanya Campbell, Theresa Wallace, and Derrick Gibson for your unconditional love and support.

Special Thanks

To my dear sister in Christ Rahwa Neguse. You have been such a blessing to me through this transformation process.

The Author's perspective

A Sister, a Poet, a Spiritual, Spoken Word, raises the frequencies of conscious minded people. It is a blue print to navigate those that deal with fear, vulnerability, emotional trauma, and to believers that may not understand that this is part of life's journey.

CONTENTS

SISTER

Beyond Measure 3
Issues of the Heart 6
"Love Zone" 7
Can't nobody Judge me! 10
Centric 11
Cougar Momma 12
"Diamond In The Rough" 13
Egocentric 15
"Forgiving the Unforgiving" 17
Ghetto Walls 19
"Hating On Me!" 20
Inside Of me 22
"Ka Trina" 23
"Poetry In Ghetto Motions" 25
Under Appraised 27
"Walking Miracle" 29

POET

A Prophetess Intro 33
Birthed Out Mother Earth 35
Caught Up 37
The Belly of the Beast 39
Ready Eagle 42
"Focus" 43
Ghetto Shadows 44
Ghetto living 45

Hate destroys hearts 47
Friend or foe 48
Hood Mentality 49
Time Warp 51
Hidden Ideals For Varieties. 53
Questions beyond the Ghetto 55

SPIRITUAL SPOKEN WORD

"A Second Chance" 59
Called Out 60
A Letter to the church 62
Crucified 64
Hate Blocks The Blessings 66
Naked 67
"No Cross No Crown" 69
No Weapons 71
"Signs" 73
Sowing Into The Kingdom 75
Strong Hold 76
"Tell My Children" 78
I Declare and I decree 80
"The Eyes of God" 83
Things to Come 85
Word 88

The Bio 91

SISTER

BEYOND MEASURE

Big round curvaceous like mother earth and her fullness thereof.
Face full as the moon scales turn up not once but twice.
Cause I realize I'm not average I'm larger than life...

I tilt the scales beyond the cosmos...
I'm light years ahead of my time...
I travel with ease through space and time...

And...

Like ecliptic shadows I cover the sun...
For it is love that over shadows me...
It consumes me like the air that I breathe...

It compliments my personality...
So don't be overwhelmed by what you see...
I'm just a big woman living in a small body...

I'm a sun on top and a moon on bottom...
Like the figure eight I have no beginning and no end...
I 'am Infinite beyond measure trace me once, then twice you got to start all over again...

My silhouette curves like an hour- glass in a figure eight motion...
Breast big as gazebo melons juicy as watermelons...
Body stretched to its limits like rubber bands...

It is the almighty that created me in this skin...
I may be small or I may be big...
I love the Queen who is housed within...

I'm beyond measure wider than all out doors...
Curves that define feminist underlying the roundness and fullness that completes me...
Well rounded without placing any limitations upon me...

Birth out the canal of the great abyss...
I tweak the scales with a twist...
I wear a double helix rainbow skirt around my waist...
Stars drapes from my wrist...

My approach has rhythm like a drum beating in the mist of the Congo's...
My roundness to my bounce beyond measure...
My sway a treasure...
My presence a pleasure...

The earth rumble's beneath my feet to announce my presence...
When I speak the atmosphere stands still at attention awaiting my next command...

And

Like dots and periods at the end of each sentence...
You have to stop and pay attention...
I'm like a centric symbol many circles revolve around me...

Incomparable to a grain of sand compared to a pebble...
I'm enormous in size beyond space and measure...
Infinite in consciousness and world wide in size...

So...

Now with all that said and done

And...

Gluttony being a sin you dare make fun of me?
I'm not easily moved by the wind...
I don't allow anything to move me...

And…

Because I'm beyond measure I don't react to everything I see…

It was human conditioning that I resisted…
I had to lift myself beyond space and measure…
It is the continuous works God placed in me…

I have arrived beyond measure…

ISSUES OF THE HEART

My heart is heavy, troubled, and confused…
Caught between man and god leaving me no choice, but to choose.
My spirit and flesh battle constantly…

Lord help me to make the right choice…

God knows my weakness.
His grace is sufficient and his love is enough…
Although I am not perfect….
The Bible says, "If we resist the devil then he shall flee from us" …

Blinded by the illusion of a superficial world…
I've mistaken the forest from the trees…
I 'm reminded things aren't always what it seems…

I question…
Can this issue bring out the best in me?

God chose me…
He holds me, molds me and consoles me…
He shapes and makes me…
God has made me wondrously…

He's given me infinite wisdom and placed his anointing upon me…
God showed me three keys to the kingdom then handed them to me…

He Says true love and happiness can only come from me…
Be obedient my child and follow my divine plan it's your destiny…

"LOVE ZONE"

How do you break down walls that has no beginning and no end?
How do you break out invisible walls from within?
I'AM Imprisoned alone and trapped in a love zone.

I sat and sat and sat in pain.

I denied myself of the love I truly deserved.
I sat in chambers of solitude I was afraid to expose the real me….

I looked at other relationships to receive self-gratification…
I felt I wasn't worthy of love and love wasn't worthy of me…
Many times I walked away from love time and time again…

I was afraid, fearful of what the outcome might be…
I sabotaged love by substituting it for premature romance.
Sacrifice; was never the issue.
Losing and loving wasn't the problem…

But…

To love and lose at the same time was just too much!
Loving over and over…

Then to lose over and over…
Love was considered a war zone…
I had to retreat…

I set up perimeters around my heart.
Forming barricades protecting the scars and injuries…
That ran deep through the channels of my heart…

I bled and I bled profusely...
Losing large amounts of blood...
My injuries ran deep as the core of mother earth extending to the ends of my soul...

They say time heals all wounds...

What about the emotional scars that never seem to go away?
What about the pain felt from day to day?

I tried to shelter myself...
I tried to safeguard my heart.
I told myself everything would be alright...

My battle scars from my past lover refused to heal although he isn't in sight...

I tried to numb the pain with all my might.
I became afraid to touch or feel anything that felt right.

Pain became my ammunition.
Hurt became my shield.
Regret became my protector.

&

Love became my fear.
I set up for boot camp in the most vulnerable areas of my heart...

I didn't know how to love...
I had declared war...
Too hurt from the past to heal...

&

Too afraid to forgive myself and move on…

A wounded soldier…
I was taken hostage a casualty of war…
I threw up the white flag I surrendered to the war…
Only to find myself chain shackled captured in a love zone…

CAN'T NOBODY JUDGE ME!

Most of you roll your eyes and some stare…
Then you turn your head and act like I'm not there…
You use judgmental jargon to justify your self-deceit…
Then there are those who are quick to fix their tongue and pass judgment over me…

Nobody can judge me or put them-selves above me…
I earn my respect as an equal…
I respect those who respect me and I have the utter-most respect for those who respect themselves…

Yet you continue to place me in a paradox of your perception…
And to think I almost wagered my self-confidence because of your prejudice preconception…
I'm constantly being appraised in your chambers of execution to appease your personal self-gratification…

Because of your asinine opinions of me…
I sat and pondered on your prejudice standards of what you call acceptable…
So you find it easier to sit there and pass judgment over me…

Judgment was set in motion the day I was conceived…
I'm much like a revelation I've already been foretold, I have yet to be seen…
To judge me would be like blasphemy you really don't know what to think about me could I be real or might I be fantasy?
I've wondered through stages of solidarity, left in doubt questioning myself because of your uncertainty of me because you feel I'm not acceptable.

You don't get that privilege can't nobody judge me!

CENTRIC

We are Polycentric people…
We are the center of the universe circling around many worlds…
We are Geo centric birth out of mother earth…

We are centered in grace…

We are Theo centric sons of God's earth…
We are Bio centric people precious as gold…
We are Concentric…

The center of the soul…

We are Heliocentric…
We revolve around the center of the sun…
We are egocentric creative beings confident in our skills…
We are eccentric peculiar people by nature…

We are retro Centric with flare fashion and style…

We are Tele O centric…
Our eyes are focused as we revolve around the universe….
We are Afro centric…
Our origins are diverse we can't be erased…

We are Centric the center in a circle….

COUGAR MOMMA

Cougar Momma,
Cougar Momma.
Afraid to get old…

Botox, face-lifts, breast implants, and booty lifts…
Just a part of your high maintance….

Ms. Cougar momma reached the peak of her climax.
Mid- life crises kicked in her sexuality is at its best…
She refuses to date anyone over thirty years old…

Best to get them in their prime so she has been told!

Question:

How long do you think this fling will last?
Once he finds a pretty young thing…
You will be history a thing of the past.

Go-ahead Ms. Cougar Momma and do what you do…
Don't let the revealing clothes, fake body, and attitude get the best of you…
I almost forgot, it's all about you…!
Go on girl, do what you do!

"DIAMOND IN THE ROUGH"

I have been reshaped in God's Glory.
Refined through the Holy spirit…

The world threw me away into a sea of shame…
God took this scuffed diamond and polished my sins away…

He saw a diamond they couldn't see…
He looked past all my flaws, which covered me…
They focused on my chips, cracks, and bruises…

They falsely accused me adding to my confusion.
They made me feel as though I was inadequate.
They wanted me to lower my standards…
As for my dreams they tried to break and shatter them…

Chip by chip I admit my spirit was broken bit by bit.
I was buried deep in the trenches…
I was mistaken for a rock a hidden jewel laying in the rough…. .

I know my value

Folks laughed, pointed, and joked along the way…

But…

God said,

The very ones who laugh will be brought to shame…

I will heal your heart and show your worth the pain inflicted will no longer hurt…
I will use your pain as a testimony…
I will reshape you then mold you from glory to glory…

Without the lessons you would have not survived the journey...

As days weeks and months went by I saw no change...
I waited for God patiently to make a way...
I cried out dear Lord how long would this process be?
I thought the Lord had forgotten about me...

He replied,
I'm glad you asked that question...

You have begun your journey...
A long time ago...
Everything I placed in you...
I've done before the foundations of the earth...

Go out in to the world my child.
I have blessed you with the poetic gift of ministries...
Tell the people, Christ my son is soon to return.
I Am the great I Am.

I have given you all you need.
You need not to worry...
My grace is sufficient for you to endure the journey...
You're my diamond in the rough...
So shall you shine for me.

I have already made provisions for the journey...
I polished you to illuminate as a testimony...

Come out my hidden treasure...
Show the world how I have restored you beyond measure...

Come from out of hiding come out the cuts you are a precious diamond...
My diamond in the Rough...

EGOCENTRIC

Egocentric folks are not going to like what I say or do…
It really doesn't matter I'm going to keep it real with you…
God resist the proud and give grace to the humble."

If God resist the proud the same goes for his righteous ones….
We walk around wearing fake military coats…
Man has honored the creature, more than his creator…
He uses excuses to justify his wrongdoing.
We've become too afraid to draw our own conclusions…

We rank ourselves by the merit system…
We numb ourselves to be preconditioned…
Banking on what people say…
Instead of what they do…

Superficial patches of rank are etched and on the sleeves and chest…

We wear badges of prestige to esteem our ego
To cover the hidden holes in our hearts…
We're so sure so full of ourselves it's all about you…
Only be left in the spotlight, not wanting to make room for no one else…

You, yourself have stood on the shoulders of giants, now you refuse to step aside…
Afraid someone else might shine?
Pride and self-image boost our mentality…
We live in an egocentric false reality

Only to look into smoked screen mirrors, and artificial images staring back at us ...
An illusional matrix designed by lies and false conclusions.

Our ego convinced us with words of reassurance saying to ourselves.... .

I got this...
I got this...
I got this...

It behooves me how we play ourselves combatively like the game of chest...
Not realizing that Father time has the last play...

Father time uses us as footstools and stepping-stones, waiting for next person to stand on our shoulders...
We boldly sport patches of authority...
Then we use time as a reference to claim our seniority...

We've become self-centered and egocentric, we're caught up in our own selfish ways...
Beyond a shadow of a doubt the more things change the more they will continue to remain the same...

"FORGIVING THE UNFORGIVING"

Most people are Quick to judge slow to forgive...
Unforgiveness the ugly beast who never wins...
We all have sat in someone's chambers waiting to be executed...
If two wrongs can't make right then who's sits in the seat of persecution...

Forgiveness strengthens the soul...
If time truly heals all wounds...
Then move on!

True forgiveness never takes no sides asking who's right or who's wrong...
We all have judged and passed judgement...
Forgiveness never blames or does it shame...
Forgiveness grants mercy to become better person some day...

Unforgiving is like a sore that never seems to heal...
Like a scab that continues to fester but never seems to peel...

Unforgiveness is a process that never cease, prideful demons of the past ruled by a stubborn beast...

The hall of blame or the hall of shame...
Demons write their names on these walls...

Unforgiveness...

A savage beast altered by the sands of time...
A form of hate ruled by the mind...
Accompanied by anger, and ruled by time...

A driving evil force too stubborn to give in…

We all have shortcomings…
We all have sinned…
Let go and let God… .

Then watch the healing begin!

GHETTO WALLS

Concrete and wood hold these wall adjacent…
Steal and cooper created these ghetto foundations…
These walls creek because they hold so much deceit.

Every layer of paint resembles monuments paying tribute to its very existence…
These walls have witnessed shattered dreams fragmentized by sexual exploration…
These walls have witnessed bloody holocausts and spiritual rituals which words are forbidden to say, so they sweat tears of silence left to drip in the moldy corner of my window pain…
They're hidden behind wallpaper, boards, and paint covering what we don't want to see because no one wants to be responsible for the blame…

These walls hold secrets to the soul they witnessed things that will never be told…
Tongues bounce off these walls sixteen times…
I said tongues bounces off these walls sixteen times edifying sounds and images left behind…

These ghetto walls are sacred like the walls in Egypt… they are the archives of ghetto hieroglyphs…
These walls are favorable to its viewers because their Stonehenge to some and stepping-stones to others.
I said their Stonehenge to some and stepping-stones to others…

"HATING ON ME!"

So…
You hating on me again…
Well I ain't mad at you…
I would hate on me too if I were you…

See God has purpose for my life…
He gave me instructions on what to do…
All I have to do is be obedient and follow through- …

What!
Now that I found God, I don't do the things I use to do…
You treat me like an outcast then ignore me and that's cool…

I have never forgotten where I came from…
It was my past that made me who I am today…
I 've dealt with haters and fake friends…

But…

This thing is bigger than you and me…
You don't understand…
God smiled on me, he marvels at the creativity he placed in me…

I'm an enigma, prodigy, a puzzle, I'm not easily figured out… I'm an oasis in the middle of the desert…
When everything around me is in sinking sand Christ is my rock on him I stand …

The hating never made a difference…
I've been blessed by the most high, favored by royalty…
Custom made by the creator a rare commodity…

Now that I understand the plan who's I am...
This thing is Spiritual it's bigger than man...
We battle not against flesh and blood so my quarrel is not with you...

I know the difference between hate, strife, and envy...
Deception is nothing but lies and trickery...
Hate gives power to the enemy...

Do you hate me because I'm favored...
They say favor isn't fair...
God's love never fails or weavers his love is unconditional even to hateful people....

INSIDE OF ME

I can't deny what's inside of me…
I've been hurt in the past I want to be set free…
I want to love again; I want my Boaz to find me…

Could it just be me?
Or…
Does he only exist inside my dreams?

Could he be before my eyes but I fail to see…
When will he reveal himself and make himself known to me…

And…

Will he be worthy of me?
Can he look over my shortcomings and all that comes with me….?
Can he deal with my imperfections and love me for me?

Will he consider my feelings or fell to neglect them?
Will he recognize the true beauty within me?
These are questions I ask inside of me…

I wrapped myself inside a cocoon…
I morphed into a butterfly waiting to be renewed…
I hid myself inside a silk cocoon praying he would seek and find me…

Yet,

I wait patiently for my Boaz…
I wait for him in certainty….
I can't ignore the process or sit to the side I've grown wings, I've transformed into a beautiful butterfly…

"KA TRINA"

A silence was approaching…
Like the Quiet storm…
Waves rolled in deep…

It's time to move on…

World winds reaching over one hundred miles per hour…
Is it another Hurricane, twister winds, or rain showers?
You knew I was coming, no one knew the time or hour…

I announced my presence before I came through…
I gave you warning after warning before I made my debut…

You saw the flood alert, flash signs, before I gave the final warnings…

Maybe you thought I would pass over…
You failed to pay attention…

You underestimated my capabilities…
You didn't make proper provisions…
I am Ka Trina…

The hurricane of destruction…

Danger ran its course as a final pursuit…
Destruction claimed many lives as terror grew…
Floodwaters held you as prisoners with no escape…
Waiting frantically for a helicopter to save the day…

My wrath pushed the south down to her precious knees.
Leaving coastlines as muddy graves and mausoleums.

I am Ka Trina...

My waters exceeded over the rims of bayous...
Causing the break down of levees spilling over inland,
Flooding marshlands and ravines...
Rain poured down immensely with a powerful force...

It was almost like the south was being punished or cursed...

Three days of terror, as death claimed its protocols for residents. Leaving disease and bacteria to claim the rest...
The word traveled fast as the storm grew near...

But...

It was too late Ka Trina was already here!

"POETRY IN GHETTO MOTIONS"

As I stand on a mountain top I look low...
I see roof tops of concrete huts...
Projects to some but home to us...

These are emotions ghetto motions...

I ascend as you descend...
Our worlds never clashing only co existing...

Our worlds join simultaneously in harmony, a figure eight motion connecting on separate axils allowing time and space to be our navigators...

These are ghetto motions signs of the times...

The almighty creator fuels our worlds...
Giving us purpose and reason to exist...
So different yet we're so alike...

We reunite continuously we're hopelessly in love...
We create a tapestry of stars in the universe...

We generate this cosmic flow of energy to conserve each other...
Change and exchange is done on a consistent bases...
We fuel and refuel each others worlds in search of answers and revelation...

Together we generate to different types of elements that can't exist without each other...
I need your fire...
You need my air...

We unite creating two different types of elements...
Our power destroys everything in sight...

I don't know maybe?
I guess we're going through-them motions
You know them ghetto motions...

UNDER APPRAISED

I'm priceless as rare as they come…
There has never been another like me, no not one…
After holding me towards the light…
You saw I was crystal clear…
There was no need for you to have any doubts or fears…

How dare you under appraise me!
Who gave you permission to determine the value of my worth…
You traded me in for a cubic zirconium and dame that hurts…

I'm exquisite creation an cold piece of work…
I'm authentic with precision….
With clarity a unique cut…
I'm a blood diamond with a pear cut.

Now what!

I'm lavender with light blue highlights…
When the sunlight beam down on me …
My under tones shine…
I illuminate adding radiance to my demeanor…
My colors change from red to pink…

You under appraised me…
You failed to take proper measurements…
You devalued a treasure…

You choose to settle for a counterfeit, when you had a diamond all the time…

You chose to chiseled with the wrong tool…
What was your mind going through?
You measured by size but underestimated my worth…

You seek to replace me, good luck!…

You should have held me towards the light and watch me radiate…

You counted the cost but failed to do the math…
You'll never find another jewel, I'm a treasure on demand, chosen by the Most-high I'AM THAT I'AM…

"WALKING MIRACLE"

I'm a walking miracle molded by the hands of God...
I'm an example a protégé...
I'm his perfect work shown on display...

When people look at me they are amazed...
I walk in the shadow of mysteries unable to be touched...
It was the love of the Most-High that kept me, love by the potter's touch
Love by the potter's touch...

God made me a priority set me aside from the majority...
A walking miracle before your very eyes...

I'm a miracle can't you see? . . .
Through God's grace his son paid the price in full for me...

I'm vivid a sight for sore eyes my dimensions run deep.
I'm unparallel in size...
Wondrously admired, respected and adored...

"Behold"

I stand before you...
A walking miracle for every man to behold
I'm a child of God not be ignored.

POET

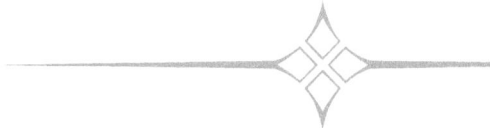

A PROPHETESS INTRO

Some say, I'm a messenger, a poet, a counselor to one's soul…

My eyes magnify the sun ten thousand times …
I have seen the rise of Pharisees and the fall of dynasties…
Could it be a gift passed on to me, or ancient eyes of prophecy…

I've looked in the eyes of men…
I have seen the reflections of the inner man's soul…
I have seen their dark shadows and naked silhouettes…

They run for cover light shines exposing their true identity…
I've read them to the essence of their souls…
I could even see through their lies truth be told…

They hide themselves between shadows because of shame…
My eyes reveal great mysteries like the cosmos unfolding around the sun.
I'm like stardust in the heavens that forms into an electrical atom creating more than one…

My spirit traveled beyond the second and third heavens…
I marvel at God's creation staring through the gates of heaven
The gates shined showing a reflection the image of my soul…

If my consciousness and soul is found guilty and convicted
I would parish and caught up in the spirit…
It's not my time I refuse to go…

Yes…

I'm God fearing as mystical as they come…
No one can fulfill my quest for revelation no not one…
My journey was tailor made for me…

God designed this project just for these ending times…
I'm here to test the soil before I plant my seeds into the land…
I'm here to sow seeds into the kingdom that's part of God's divine plan…

My seeds must be of Grade A soil…
If I sow too soon, the harvest will spoil…
I'm not here to read a soul.

I'm simply here to say
I have arrived look out for me towards the sun…

The ending of times is at hand and Revelation has begun…
As a representative in pursuit of my mission…
I shall arise by the mighty hand of God.

I' am seated in my rightful position…
As a prophetess heir to the Almighty God and visionary of the kingdom…
My mission is to sow seeds of wisdom by warning God's people, and prepare his children for the kingdom…

I'm an ambassador, an heir of God's kingdom…

BIRTHED OUT MOTHER EARTH

I was formed from the dust and chiseled from my mother's womb...
I was baptized and washed in the crimsoned tides....

We are compatible generically inclined...
My soil is fertile and rich I reproduce as well as multiply...
My treasures fall from the heavens I reproduce in abundance to all mankind...

Mother Earth's first born...
Not only did I receive my mother's blessings...
I also inherited her earthy treasures...

I'm birth from diamonds minerals and exotic stones out my mother's womb...
She bleeds symphonies of oils and fossil fuel...
Not only do I have evidence, I'm living proof...

I help to sustain life beyond measure...
I reproduce jewels as well as treasures...

Mother Earth Mother cradle all humanity, I see as she sees...
The human civilization began with her, but man's seed belongs to me ...
The first tree man planted rose in the garden of Eden...
Mother earth produces the greatest quantity of resources from within....

She produces more than enough resources to feed the entire hemisphere...
She's blessed to reproduce in abundance and do so abundantly...

With provision came division, I have always existed...

one country...
One continent...

One people...
One world
I'm Africa birthed out of mother earth...
I 'am Africa, Africa and is me...

CAUGHT UP

I was caught up…
I lost focus…
I was so into your worth…
Yet I neglected myself…

Now,

I can't say you took my power…
Hell I gave it away…
Only because I thought you were worthy…

So…

I boosted your esteem with praise…
I wanted you to see the big picture and all you had to gain…
In the end it cost me emptiness, worry, and pain…

I was there when all we had was each other…
I showed you the endless possibilities you couldn't see…
I encouraged you to stand strong no matter how bad things may have seemed…

I prayed for you at night and asked God to make a way…
I believed God would make a way…
I was the one to give you a helping hand when no one else would help…

You took the ball and ran with it…
I guess that's what you were suppose to do…
How soon do we forget….
I was there when so-called friends turned their backs on you…

You're able to stand on your own feet…
I guess you only needed me for the time being…
What you fail to see…
You were being positioned for a reason not for a season…

THE BELLY OF THE BEAST

Juices of corruption oozes out her cracks
Her belly now leaks…
No longer holding us captive, by blinding us with false illusions…

Her water bag has broken…
The truth is now exposed…
Mysteries are unfolding…
Revelation has gone forward…

Our reality has been hidden and stolen.
Lies have been traded off as tokens.

The beast has been pregnant in travail for much too long.
The second coming of Christ must come his will be done.

The beast uses tactics of dominance and injustice, implanting artificial insemination, giving a swollen appearance, making her belly appear larger than life.
After falsely accusing us of being the baby daddy without taken a D.N.A sample…

&

Instead of singing a birth Cert…
We signed a Death Cert…

The belly has mixed whipped, and churned, the truth into butter.
The belly growls with hunger pains waiting to regurgitates off its own toxic waste…
Then passes off corruption as Social Justice…

The belly holds no walls for our protection it serves its own...
If there's no justice for me there's no justice for us.

We are the one's who suffer from the abortions brought on by the breast...

And

Because no body went in and preformed a DNC...
No one removed the dead fetus...
No body scraped her wounds and because of that.
Her insides begin to rotten, and decay tumors starts to fester...

Bureaucracy has turned into cancer...
Society is bleeding from her ass and no one can stop her flow...
The blood of the people is being wiped from hand to hand

We waged ourselves by buying into a false perception of what a dream should be...

&

Because we missed the vision it's time to reach down into your spirit...
All the signs are there stop, pay attention and like Martin Luther King, not only did he have a dream he also had a vision...

How long will we sit in silence and settle for mediocrity...
We set up our own chamber of execution causing us to waiver from righteousness we settle for justice...

Just as long as it doesn't affect us personally, it's okay with us...
The agenda is to tare down and infuse its position of authority...
Using tactics, dominance, and inferiority...

&

If you are a minority then you are not a priority...

Deception and scrutiny are the twins that are held in her wound...

&

Like a mother's true nature she will protect them at all cost...

READY EAGLE

I'm an eagle…
I'm majestic I sour on high…
I'm an eagle I'm ready to fly…

Buzzers, vultures, and parasites have devoured my flesh for much too long…
My feathers have been ruffled because of numerous storms…
My wings have been clipped by fear and doubt…
Time to spread my wings so this eagle can sour about…

I'm ready to sour gracefully in the air . . .
I see heaven and earth parallel…
I'm ready to look low and fly high…

I'm ready to form dust clouds in the sky…
I can see my adversaries approach with my keen site…
I can swoop down and eat my pray in one bite…

I'm an eagle…
I'm ready sour . . .
I'm ready to discover the possibilities and much, much, more…

"FOCUS"

Set backs, delays, and disappointments…
Everything under the sun…
Focus obstacles can stagnate growth…

Issues may arise like the sun…
Or…
Perhaps they may burn up like a phoenix waiting to be reborn…

To lose focus is like a women scorn…
She's never really over it she simply finds other ways to hold on…

Stay focused centered, grounded, hold fast don't be easily moved by what you see, focus set your sights on the possibilities. Never become impatient, partial, or naïve…

Don't look to the left or to the right…
You might loose focus you might loose sight…
Push forward full speed ahead…

Refuse to be stopped, distracted or discouraged along the way…
The good you do will pay off some day…

Focus on what you set out to do…
Not only will you be an inspiration…
You will be an accomplishment too…

Your hard work will be rewarding…
You could inspire someone else too…
Stay consistent and focus…

Don't be afraid to be you!!!

GHETTO SHADOWS

I've seen the shadows reflecting from the streetlights…
That's when my eyes were open to the fact that spirits roam the ghetto late night…

I've seen the souls that tread these concrete places …
Restless weary souls in search of their maker…
These lost souls congregate giving life and death relations…
They tend their post patiently in waiting their redemption…

My eyes have seen the shadows lurking in the night…
There was a strange presence felt when no one was in sight…
I heard cries and whispers in the atmosphere; I saw the shadows when no one was there…

I felt the cold chills, which makes your hair stand on your head…
So no one…

I mean no one!
Can't tell me…
That shadows aren't there…
That they don't exist or linger through the air…

GHETTO LIVING

There was a time when ghetto living was exciting to me.
Not only did I live in the ghetto…
The ghetto lived in me.

I was caught in a Ghetto mentality.
I refused to face reality…
I looked at life as a technicality…

I feared what others expected…
Afraid to be rejected…
I still wanted to be respected…

I had to re-evaluate and reconsider what's important to me…
I had to change my mind setting and realize…
I live in the ghetto; 8the ghetto doesn't live in me!!!

I took charge and made me a priority…
I raised my hands to God and walked into my Authority…

I refused to accept the anguish before me…
I looked through the eyeglasses of opportunities.
I saw a bright future for me.

I saw the endless possibilities…
I took advantage of the ghetto…
I made it work for me…

I refuse to be blinded by the things that were seen…
I turned my nightmare into a wonderful dream…
It was the ghetto lessons that shaped me…

The experiences that made me…

&

The trials that saved me...
Even through all the hurt and the pains...
I still wouldn't change a thing...
Experience made me who I am today...

I found shelter from the rain...
I stood strong through heartaches and pain...

&

Because of that I stand before you today...
I transformed myself into a new state of being...
To experience true freedom...

I released what was inside of me...
I realized the battle wasn't on the streets...
It was within me...

&

Because of lack of resources...
I couldn't see the forest from the trees...
My situation made it hard for me to believe ...

I took the issues of the ghetto...
I took notes and inventory on everything I seen...

I called things as they are not...
So shall they be...
I discovered my hidden power...
I declared and decreed...
I refused to let the ghetto mentality get the best of me...

&

I'm so proud to say, I once lived in the ghetto the ghetto no longer lives in me!

HATE DESTROYS HEARTS

Past relationships and painful memories had me locked in a nutshell.
No one knows my pain so what the hell.
I kept it to myself…
I suppress the pain I felt…

It seemed easier for me to hold it all in…
I numb myself so I couldn't feel.
Like a lump of coal under the hottest amount of pressure I crystallize…
How do I turn this heart of coal into flesh?
How do I stabilize?

Set backs and disappointments grew in the chambers of my heart.
I used time as a vehicle to cope…
The issues of life grew like weeds…

And…

Instead of plucking the weeds up from the roots…
I cut it short only to find that the same issues had rose up once again…
Hate started to grow like vines around a picket fence…

I late grew intensely vines began to locked and Intertwine.
I became wrapped up losing myself in the issues of life…
The more hate grew it destroyed my flow of life…
My blood no longer flow freely, it evaporated like vapors of water…

Hate became my main consumer…
My heart became stony ground…

Hardening my arteries…
Blood no longer flow…

Don't let hate destroys the heart only to leave a hollow hole…

FRIEND OR FOE

You say I'm your friend but your quick to put me down...
You talk about me behind my back...
Call me names and clown...

You use my weakest points to justify your deceit...
How dare you smile in my face laugh and joke with me...
As long as we're okay and I comply with all your rules...
Just as long as we see eye to eye everything is cool...

The minute I disagree...
You feel threatened not knowing what to do...
So you compromise our relationship...
You try to play me as a fool...

Friend or foe...
You chose the rules...
We could agree to disagree, but no!
Now you want to catch an attitude?

Once all said and done rather I'm right or wrong...
Rather we agree or not or if I should be appalled or delighted it should change the love for me...
Our respect for each other should have made us stronger...
All because we don't agree, you choose to distance yourself further, and further...

Friend or foe, which one are you?
I guess your one in the same so there no need to choose...

HOOD MENTALITY

The hood reality was getting the best of me . . .
The more I resisted the more the hood continued to fight…
No matter what I did the hood wouldn't let me out!

I was consumed by the hood harsh realities…

Until one day…

The hood spoke to me and said… .
I see you're trying to escape my raft and my harsh realities…
Contrary, to your beliefs and all that is negative in the hood…
There's two sides to every story so don't be dismay by what you see . . .
Come journey with me…

Negative and positive each perception lies within the walls of me…
I can be your best friend or your worst enemy.
You choose who you want me to be…

Headstones or milestones are carved from me . . .
I could lift you up or bury you six feet deep…
Who did you say you want me to be?

Running away was never the answer…
You still had to report to me…
Now, I'm not trying to stunt your growth or shackle you in chains…

10 years of living in this concrete prison…
Girl your debt is paid!
I'm releasing you to tell a story about the realities of the hood . . .

Run girl, run don't you dare walk away!
But...
Hold on girl, there's just one other thing....
Don't you ever forget from where you came!

TIME WARP

Arise! Arise!
Children from the 60's and 70's time to wake up!
You got caught up in the eighties and nineties now you're stuck…
Time has raped you from your future…
Father time has left you pregnant your baby is due…

Dreams and aspirations has been pushed down like cotton balls in an aspirin bottle…
The contractions are too strong the pain is too much…
Father time left you with a destiny child…
Now you're stuck…

Young forever hold on to that thought
Instead of making time a privilege you made it a pleasure…
Now you turn your head to the sky in search of something better…

And…

Because you didn't make good use of time…
Time used you…
Now that you're released from your time warp…
You don't know what to do…

Whatcha know bout dem 80's smoking weed and having babies?

Yeah…

Whatcha know bout dem 90's
Kickin, it ridin, and high siding?

As the decades crept on so did father time…
All that's left are collections of memos and memories…
Like Cumulonimbus clouds time drifted away…

Instead of strategizing now you're apologizing…
Dreams and ambitions got tossed to the wind…
You placed time on scales but it held no weight…

You compared time to a grain of salt…
You tasted the sweet grains of time…
Only to find that sweet father time turned into salt pillars…

Your mouth thirst for water praying father time quench your thirst…
As for father time well he can be a blessing or a curse…
You didn't seize time.
Now time has you under siege…

You got stuck into a time warp best believe…

Time is like games of hang man…
You fill in the blanks…
You used time without no discretion…
Leaving you hanging with no balance…

Ropes couldn't buy time or give you leverage…
Like they say.…
Give a man enough rope eventually he will hang himself…

HIDDEN IDEALS FOR VARIETIES.

I 'm Hidden Ideals for varieties acronym H.I.V.
I go undetected for years you can't see me...
I run rampant giving flu like symptoms I infect your bloodstream and wage attack on my victims...

I infect them killing my victims slowly...
I scout new victims then hunt them down like prey...
&
Before they know it full-blown A.I.D.S.
I don't discriminate, I don't die, or divide, I multiply...
   Without the use of a condom, I get stronger every time...

My seeds insidious, my strands infectious...
I mutate then emulate cells that fight me...
I destroy and dominate cells that fight against me...

I have declared all out war...
My mission is to break down the immune system then ultimately destroy...

You can take medications and holistic treatments to keep me out the way, before it all said and done...
I will destroy you anyway...

To the young teens having unprotected sex...
You have better chances playing Russian roulette...
The odds are against you...
They aren't in your favor...

So check that promiscuous behavior...

You've over rated and underestimated time for sex...
The average time falls short from three to ten minutes...

Yet it only takes me seconds to complete my mission...
What.....
This isn't what you envisioned?

Just like my victims they had all good intentions...
I attack without warning...
I don't ask for permission...

My attacks are settled...
My approach is abrupt...

Flip a coin heads or tales sorry you just ran out of luck...
You called my bluff then tried to play me...
Not only do I destroy lives...
I kill dreams and steal destinies...

That condom you disregarded was for your protection.
I'm the virus with no love can't you see...
I seek out all races and ages, I don't discriminate no not me...

Hidden Ideals for varieties Acronym H.I.V

QUESTIONS BEYOND THE GHETTO

When I talk to my friends, I ask what do see in their future…
Where do they see themselves ten years from now?
Where do they want to be?

Most talk about money, sex, and luxuries…
Surely you you're not going to settle this
Do you see yourself ow business, establishment?

They look at me with angrier as if I'm their adversary…

As I look out my window…
I see acres and acres of concrete huts…
It puts me in the mind-set of slavery…
When slavery once had rule over us…

I ask them…
You do realize you live on a plantation?
Only there's been concrete added making it more accommodating.

Wooden shacks molded into concrete forming huts…
And…
Because we're low income…
Doesn't mean we have to put up with all kinds of stuff…
Walls and cabinets filled with roaches dust and decay…
We still keep telling ourselves it's okay…

I know one-day things will get better…
A better life awaits beyond the ghetto!!!

SPIRITUAL SPOKEN WORD

"A SECOND CHANCE"

God has giving me a second chance not by measure.
But…
By Grace.

I've been shown favor by the most high…
He said live my child it's not your time to die…
It's no secret puzzle or prodigy; my father has plans for me… .

I've been broken down to be built up…
Brick by brick-block by block…
God's grace has placed in me his perfect strength…

A second chance he granted me….
He has shown me endless possibilities…
To those who receive much, much more is required….
God wrote a new plan he set the standards higher…

He promised to keep me, and never forsake or abandon me…
He chastises me, scolds me, and consoles me…
He informs me but never ignore me…

One more chance I cried out of fear…
He heard my cries…
He saw my tears…

When life was at it's worst despite the devil's plan…
God gave me strength he reassured me he had a plan…
He held me up when I couldn't stand…

I know beyond a shadow of a doubt God rewards with second chances…

CALLED OUT

You have been called out by grace placed under my holy mantel...
I will never give you more than you can handle...
My grace is sufficient...

I make my selection and choose them at random...
To serve any other Gods, would be a travesty a scandal.

I make my selection through confession...
I require repentance of your sins that you will be forgiven...
I called You Out!!!
To cleanse your heart then break down the foul
ground from within...

My spirit speaks in silence, with utterance and patience my covenant is
declared by my decree in reference to my ordinances...

Not only have you been called out you've been chosen...
I have placed you under the veil and covered you for my prevision...
I called you out to do my will.
You made your choice; I've made the final decision...
I have reserved and preserved you time and time again...

I have called you into destiny for such a time as this...

My spirit will be exalted you dare not to quench...
I have called you out to do my will...
My quotas will be fulfilled...
My return draws near...

You have been predestined….
Your praise and honor belongs to me…
I created you for my purpose…
Can't you see?

Not only do I give you life, I hold your destiny…
You have been called out from the mantle…
You have been ordain, renamed, and engrafted into me…

I called you out with a purpose in mind…

You are my flawless design…
Complete the journey while there's time…
I shall show you miracles, wonders, and signs…

I have called you out in these last days and times…
I' am Ahayah I AM that I Am…
You may choose to run but you can't hide…

You have been called from the mantel into forbearance…
I have given you keys to the kingdom as a reward for your Inheritance…

My remnant has been sought out…
& You have been called out!!!

A LETTER TO THE CHURCH

You have written me off...
You have signed the final divorce of decree...
You have taken the sanity out of holiness...

You have taken your intimacy from me...
You were my son's first love...
You were engrafted though me...
You sold me out for corruption, profits and deceit...
You told lies of destruction, you uncircumcised me then performed your own abortion...

Now I leave you alone.
To saturate in the juices of your own corruption...
I have given you more than glass stain windows, pole pits and periodic prayer sessions...

I have given you inhabitance to the world yet you refuse to grab it...
I have exalted you high above all nations...
Yet, the world has captured you under its persuasion...

Time and time again, I have taken you into my hands like dough...
You have been shaped, molded, and kneed like bread...
In preparation to serve my people their daily bread...

Yet you serve them commentary crumbs, which have fallen from the throne's dining room table. Like hungry foolish dogs my children sloop up the bits and pieces because they don't know any better...

You send my children away to die from starvation and spiritual deprivation...

There's no way out because you have sold out...
My judgment have gone forth my children have been governed to their rightful positions...
You stated your demise and failed to up hold my ordinance...

The notion has been set forth...
You filed your final petition of decree...

It is my standards you have failed to meet...
The heavens are silent the windows have been shut...
The first and second heavens are closed...

It is only through faith, the holy-spirit and prophetic discernment...
My children will receive knowledge, instructions and warranting...
Those who remain to take their position must seek ye the kingdom by Renouncing man's religion...
Governments have been established to meet proper provisions
Therefore the notion has been set forth.
You've made your requests known unto me.

I've rendered the final judgment.
And...
So it shall be!

CRUCIFIED

You have burdened me down with your words of crucifixion…
On bended knees I fell to the ground, you paid no attention…
I carried my own cross so you could complete your mission…
I was beaten with many strips…
I died for your redemption…

You spat, pointed, and laughed at me, while I hung on that rugged cross…
You placed a crown of thrones on my head as blood dripped from my nose to my mouth…
I never mumbled one word, I never cried, shouted, or fussed…
You pierced me on my sides then slashed wounds into my flesh…
You nailed my feet and hands to the cross I never asked them to take them out…
I had to die so you could live…
There was no other way…
I had to pardon you for your sins…
It was never about my death I came to save my people from their sins…

I'AM the son of the Almighty God heir to the great I'AM through Shekinah's glory I rose again…
My crucifixion always had an intention…
Because of me you now have a birth right to the kingdom…
My father made me the ultimate sacrifice…
I made you my privilege…
I came so you may have life and have it more abundantly…
To this day you continue to nail me to the cross and persecute me…
You spit in my face lie and deny me…
Your words are tainted and your tongue is marked…
You speak deceiving lies your far from truth…
You look to heavens for answers I'm the proof…
You crucified me then walked away as I hung, on the cross for you…
I told you I'm the son of God you believe me not, the way has been paid;
Yet you continue to slander my name.
You claim to be a baptized believer in me…
You took the oath of communion in remembrance of me…
You crucify me over and over each time you disobey my father…
Every time you fail to give God thanks and honor…
When you fuss, fight, and mistreat each other…
When you can't forgive your fellow brother…
Before I left the world I looked up to the heavens; I said father it is finished, all my suffering was put to an end…
I came that you may have eternal life, to save you from your sins…
Why must you choose to crucify me time, and time, and time again?

HATE BLOCKS THE BLESSINGS

Are you still hating on me that's a shame?
I'm not mad at you...
You see God has a plan for my life...

He gave me instructions on what to do...
All I have to do is be obedient and do what he tells me too...
What so you mean to tell me
Now that I have a renewal of mind and I'm on top of my game...
You treat me as an outcast I'm a true friend in need yes indeed...
I never forgot where I came from, it was my past that made me who I'AM today...
Dealing with fake people and so called friends, rooted in jealousy and envy from within...

The hate cycle is madness it never seems to end...

God's never ceases to amaze me...
I've been blessed by the Almighty God and favored by royalty...
You see this thing is bigger than you and me...

If I didn't I understand God's plan and I were you...
My heart would be full of hate and envy too...
There's no difference, God loves us all the same...

Only Christ can heal a broken heart and free you from your pain...
Let go the hate , then watch your blessings come your way....

NAKED

You stand before me naked…
You have looked on other Gods…
I am a jealous God…
You have committed adultery in my presence with no regards…

Now you stand before me naked…

You cover yourself in shame, then you drape yourself in garments made from ratchet materials of this world…
I took your measurements personally…

I've selected your materials…
Your garments were tailor made especially for you…

I matched you in the finest threads…
Stitch by stitch woven by woven…
I selected you to spread the gospel…
It is you that I have chosen…

Now you stand before me naked…

What happened to the garments…
The one's so eloquently made?

I equipped you with apparel for each season…
I've prepared your rain gear in case you might need it…
You sold me out, casting lots auctioning me off to the highest bidder…

I've watched you lower your standards, accepting bribes and bids along the way…
How you used worldly possessions and monetary compromises to feed your greed and ego…

How dare you raise a bloodstain-tainted banner claiming your representing the kingdom?
Is it not so that itchy ears and bottomless bellies have taken counsel of the hearts of many?
Instead of waiting for my next command you took the church in your own hands…

Because you were impatient and blinded by what you see…
You lost sight and failed to put your full trust in me…
I've seen how you indulged in worldly treasures…
Time after time you put other Gods in front of me…
Gods of greed, lust, compromise, judgment, and hate have invaded the hearts and consumed the minds of my people…

I've watched you whore my body to other Gods…
You conducted side deals and manipulated the gospel, denying me like the Sadducees in roman times…

Because of you and your demise…
The hearts of my people are waxing cold, burning with unquenchable desires…
You've corrupted the hearts of my children, and taken my name in vain….
They bring their burnt tithes and offerings to cover up their sins…

Causing them to miss the mark of the high calling…

How dare you stand before me naked?
What do you have to say for yourself?
I'm bigger than manna, silver, and gold…
I am the God of all creation haven't you been told?

"NO CROSS NO CROWN"

I often wondered why life is sometimes so cruel?
Why must people suffer?
Why must they do the things they do?

I asked the Almighty a question...
He replied as gentle as an ocean breeze...
My child...

I gave every man the freedom to choose as he pleases...
Every man decides his own destiny...

What ever choice he decides, rather it be wrong or right...
Let each man be responsible...
Let each man pay his price...

I then heard him say...
My child no cross no crown...
I test my children to see what they're made of...

Will they break under pressure when it seems there's
No way out...

I heard him say three times...
No cross no crown...
No cross no crown...
No cross no crown...

Those who have faith, in my word...
Stand on solid ground...

You must endure the bad to get to the good...
All of this is done for my glory, your experience might give faith and hope to some and to others as a living testimony...

You must be tried and refined...
Placed under the hottest pressure...
It is then and only then...

I can reshape you and bring out the perfect treasure...
It is then I can weigh your works...
Then size you up for measure...

Will you be worthy to wear a crown of treasure... ?

NO WEAPONS

God's elect, elite...

G.P.O.L. God's people on the frontline...
I have top-secret plans written by the Almighty hands...
He gave specific instructions on what to do...
He said take back all that the enemy has stolen from you...

"God said"
Lay low my child and stay in the trenches...
My son won the battle for your redemption...
You must use your weapons to endure the race...

My grace is sufficient I will keep you safe...

Use the word as your sword of protection...
Use faith as a compass knowing I'll always make a way...
Use prayer as a shield from day to day...

Use worship and praise as your letters and messages to the kingdom...
Use repentance to break strongholds by destroying yokes for spiritual freedom...
Use fasting as your spiritual acid to keep the flesh under submission...

Use meditation to keep the tongue from destroying the vision...
Use the breastplate of righteousness to shield you from an impure heart...
Use the helmet of righteousness to protect you from unclean thoughts...

The weapons are not used for carnality...
Their used to protect your spirituality...

I'm on the battlefield now...
Man down! Man down! Man down!
I retreat, I run for cover!

I'm under satanic attack.

The enemy has formed nuclear warheads, scud missiles, and chemical warfare against me.

His plans are to take me out and destroy me...

He has set up weapons of destruction all around me...
His troops spy and conspire to overtake my defeat...
He slides through shadows and attack me in my sleep...

He shifts shapes from time and places...
He brings up the past...
He reminds me of familiar faces...

He uses fear and doubt as tools to keep me inferior...
He uses tactics and lies to implement his demise...
He uses tools of deception to steal my inheritance...

Back up devil you have no rights here!!!
I know your plans are to lie, cheat, and steal...
I've been instructed, to kill!!!

"SIGNS"

The ending of time, the dawning of dusk.

God said…

In the last days he would pour his spirit upon all flesh…

Man must be obedient and follow God's commandments time is running out man needs repentance…

The iniquities of the world is coming to a final judgment…
God has given man free will as well as abundance…
God forbid that no man should parish, he offers the kingdom of righteousness which is his inheritance…

Time after time God has given us warnings and signs
We're the ones who choose to be blind;
because of lack of knowledge we tolerate deception only to see one side…

Man has made himself a priority…
He has no respect for God's authority…
The world will see who has the seniority…

If Christ doesn't come back soon…
We all be doomed…

Signs, Signs, Signs, of the times…

His children know his signs, he prepared us for these perilous times…

We will continue to fight the good fight.
Use our spiritual weapons with all our might…

Although,

We battle not with flesh and blood but with principalities in high places

The world shall see greater trials and greater tribulations…
Wait, Watch, and listen…
The world will soon see!!!

These are the darks days revealing's, tribulations the signs of the times…

SOWING INTO THE KINGDOM

I could have sown my seeds of wisdom into fortune and fame...

But...

Why sow living seeds in a dying world that is fading away...
I know what the ancient scrolls said...

I'm wise enough to know that sowing reaps a harvest...
A wise man prepare early, he stores for the next season...

But...

This goes deeper than a physical manifestation...
This law holds truth since the beginning of creation...

Sowing and reaping are dominant principals keeping balance and order...

Sowing destroys the yokes of poverty, by stopping evil forces from stealing the majority...

Like a farmer who plants a crop of wheat he plants with expectation to sow from what he reaps ...
The laws remain the same when you sow into the kingdom...

STRONG HOLD

Everyone's talking at the same time, too many voices, now hush!
Caught up in a battle, the spirit war against the flesh...
The heart is heavy, troubled, and confused...
Caught between the world and the word of God, confused which to choose...
We can't serve two masters, we must choose...
We battle with the things that have strongholds...

It's about God it was never about us...
Have no fear in the creator he holds our destiny...
We been lost, deceived, and misguided along the way...
We battle with strong holds from day to day...

Thank God for his son he paid the way...
God gave his son to die for you and me...
Choosing anything else would be a catastrophe...

We can't let strongholds shackle us down...
No more will sin have me tied up and bound...
No longer can we sit in silence and let the devil lead us astray...
Humble yourself on bended knees...
We are strong but the battle is within...

God said, I set Life and death before you...
Choose, who will you serve? so let it be said so let it be done!...
I've given you free will the choice is up to you...
Take heed to my love letter, you've been instruction what to do...?
You can't serve two masters on this day you must choose... .

Yes I'm afraid of disappointing the Almighty but I also fear loosing my soul.

Because,...

We've been blinded by illusions of this superficial world…
The enemy tries to confuse us, our vision is sometimes distorted…
We're reminded things are not always what they seem…
These are the strong holds we battle to be set free…

The enemy can't make me doubt I 'am free…
Our father always take care of what's his.
Despite what the enemy may want you think he hasn't forgotten about me or you…..

Those who Christ set free is free indeed!!!

"TELL MY CHILDREN"

Write this message for my children to heed…
Tell them their lives are precious they must endure the journey…

I test my children to give them strength…
Will you go astray because things didn't go your way…

Realize everything done has a divine purpose…
My children may not always understand….
I have a divine plan…
I 'AM ALFA AND OMEGA,
THE beginning AND THE END,
I AM THAT I AM!

My commands and ordinance set the standards for man….
Redemption is part of my plan…
Those that are born again of the water and the spirit, are my chosen vessels they understand the kingdom…

I have given my children wisdom foolish to the average man…
Obey my commandment is what I demand….
Love your brother are requirements I command…

My plans never change…
I am the almighty I never sleep or slumber….
Cleave to me my child and fret not over evil people…

This world has nothing to offer but heartache and pain…
The iniquities of this world will come into judgment one day…

My children fret not your heart…
You need not to gloat or pain…

For…

I will fight the good fight until you return unto me someday…

I DECLARE AND I DECREE

I decree and I declare my authority.....
I'm taken back all that the enemy has stolen from me.....

I've been traumatized and deceived into espionage.....
Sabotage was the plan, I chose to retreat.....

The enemy held my blessings he refused to release.
Due to the fact my convictions ran deep.....
Treason was the reason I signed my Declaration of Decree.....

I cleansed myself in the blood of the lamb.....
Then baptized myself in spiritual essences.....
The enemy tries to blot out my Declaration and denounce my Decrees.....

I had to raise the bloodstain banner to be set free.....
My blessings were held in captivity.....

Strong holds, became my shackles fear began to set in.....
I found myself being tortured by the enemy from within.
He used lies and deceit...
He used tactics and doubt to stagnate my beliefs.....

Faith and prayer was the only way to demise his defeat.....

Satan whispered in my ear with lies.....
He tried to convince me not believe.....

I fast and prayed.....

I refused not to believe.....

That's when I announced my declaration... .

I refuse to let the enemy lie and steal... .

God said name your seeds then decree... .
You can't reap a harvest in a field of weeds... .
Sift though your soil then plant your seeds... .

You can't decree what you don't believe... .
Neither can you reap harvest if you don't name your seeds... .
The blessing starts with a vision of faith.
So keep your eyes on me... .

I have given you authority... .
Take the proper steps and trust in me... .
I have placed a higher standard in thee... .

You need not to settle for mediocrity... .
The world is your oyster your loyalty belongs to me... .
I gave you authority to trample over scorpions like the dust beneath your feet... .

God said... .
You are victorious, no longer will you listen to lies and settle for defeat...
No need not to apology or feel intimidated, no longer are you under the enemy's persuasion... .

I lifted my hands to the heavens giving God thanks and praises thanking him for everything he has done for me...
It was all in God's timing before my dreams became reality.
Delayed blessing don't mean denied... .
I exercise my authority from up high... .

It's wasn't enough to declare and decree... .
Speak the invisible into existence., I declared and decreed, I gave it to God, I waited, watched to see...

When all was said It was done, I held fast to my beliefs.... .
I will give you the desires of thy heart.
Don't be discouraged by what you see... .
I'm an awesome God I specialize in possibilities... .

I can erase, remove, wait, and cease... .
I will step up or step back... .
I will sit silence wait, watch and see how you react... .
I' am not a man, I can not lie, nor do I take back... .
If my word shall return void unto me all creation will revert back void... .
The prayers of the righteous prevail much... .
Yokes must be destroyed to break the generational curse... .

All that you desire has been declared and decreed... .
Seek the kingdom and all will be added unto thee... .

"THE EYES OF GOD"

My soul ascended far past orbit…
Out through-the great Abyss…
Far pass the sun, beyond the Milky Way…

My eyes saw galaxies unfold then divide twelve times over…
I discovered patterns of stars, beams of solar lights as fire appear before me blinding me with its glorious glare…

I closed my eyes then opened them in a split second…
I looked upon a blue lagoon…
The waters shimmered under the sun, sparkling like diamonds…

The waters soothed me…
My soul danced vastly in the springs…
Giving me a sense of rejuvenation and vitality…
Soothing the very essence of my soul…

The waters warmed me…. .
Then comforted me at the same time…
Giving me a sense of peace and clarity…
I then delighted myself into the waters…

Suddenly,

A drop of water fell from up above…
A whirlpool took on immense speed.
I tried to keep a float…
I got drug down by the under currents…

I found myself at the bottom of the Lagoon...
Sitting patiently on a rock...

Then,

In an instant, the same current that drug me under pushed me up to the top of the wreath...
It was then I realized that, I had not swam in a Lagoon at all...

I had swam in the eye of God...

THINGS TO COME

I'm realistic to simplistic in every word I speak.
I heed my words as a warning, not only for you but also for me…
If there wasn't a logical reason…
There would be no need for me to deliver this message…
In hopes you will receive it…

If God didn't enlighten my path and take my hand…
I would be lost misguided…
Unable to see the bigger plan…

I'm a visionary…
I see beyond reality….
What I see don't determine my destiny…

I can be of help if you need me…

Provide wisdom if you receive it…

And

Faith if you believe it…

Not only will I be a guide to you…
I will reveal, revelation, and truth…
Some may looked in doubt and dismay…
Some may even question every word that I say…

Then there's your nonbeliever's and that's okay…
But those who discern will feel what I have to say…

The world will be called, under a mandated into one world order...
Super powers will unite together to fulfill its quota...

The systems of the world will be loosed, bound, and shaken...
The world must prepare it's self for a rude awaking...
Now that the systems are broken, the truth is being spoken...

Mysteries and secrets unfolds so that prophecy is told...

Sickness will run ramped in epidemic portions...
Pesticides and famine will also rule the land...
This is all apart of the divine plan...

There will be earthquakes, tsunamis, and hurricanes in remote parts of the earth...

Laws of nature will be abolished from the second heavens to mother earth...

Terrors will dance across the floors of the blue deep...
Mother Earth's face is cracking Her foundation is not stable...
her legs no longer can stand she's become disabled...
She lie like the dust beneath her feet...
She reproduces, but she's becoming frail and weak.

You've polluted the air with Chem trails her egos system awkward, unbalanced, her polar caps have shifted and repositioned...
Fish and birds are dying from poisons and pollution, they will soon become in extinction non-Existence.
Mother earth is in her worst condition...

Shame on you, peeking under Mother earth skirt tale, you raised her skirt over her head...
You've beaten her, raped, forsaken, her than left her for dead....
She has been mistreated and falsely accused.

In time Man will close his eyes shaking his head in disbelief…
He will run for escape and find no relief…

The financial powers will be shaken and broken…
In preparation for the second coming…
For those who hear me take notes and pay attention.

For judgment shall come so seek your redemption…
Nations will fall God Kingdom will be built up…
That's just the beginning of what's to come…

WORD

I realize your minds are weary; you're searching for a word…
You need a word to fulfill the void of emptiness…
A word to sooth the soul…

The mind, body, and spirit are adjacent.
So you run for a safe haven.
You need a word of protection…

Cause you're afraid of your own reflection…
You are consumed with doubt…

Well here I am to reveal what it's all about?
You stacked up fears like cobblestones…
Now the odds are stacked against you…

You tried to create foundations out of rocky places…
Your house collapsed you weren't stable.
Now you seek for a word…

But hold on…

You turned milestones into stepping-stones of fear…
You build stone houses denouncing yourself…
Screaming echoes bounce off the walls of hollow caves…

Sounding like soft whispers that are lost in the night…

You run trembling in fear…

But tell me?

How many fiery darts has your tongue flung in the atmosphere…
Tell me how many eyes dropped tears caused by words you held dear?
Everyone wants a word but no one wants to be corrected or reproved…

We all want a make me feel good word but no one wants to hear the truth…

If I didn't keep it real then my purpose can't be fulfilled.

The word of God is quick, powerful, and shaper than a two-edged sword, piercing even to the dividing asunder of the soul and spirit, and of the joints and marrow, and is a discerner of thoughts and intents of the heart…

The word is intrinsic, specific, powerful, and significant…

Your ears may not want to hear the truth but…

You long for it…

Your flesh craves for it…

Your soul delights in it…

&

You're a spiritual being ….
I'm not afraid to say it…
I'm here to spread the word, plant seeds, giving knowledge, and truth…

After I make my peace and spread the word, the rest is up to you…
Words are powerful they light the path and lead the way…
That's why we must be mindful of the words we choose to say…

You wanted a word, did I tear you down or did I build you up?
Did it open your eyes or add to your hurt…
If you spare the rod you spoil the child…

If one is never corrected he never knows the value of his worth…
I guess the old saying remains the same…
They say the truth hurts…

THE BIO

Self-Discovery | At the age of twelve, Trina was inspired by her middle school teacher who took interest in her writings. Her teacher noticed Trina's gift of writing and encouraged her to fulfill her potential. Trina began writing personal poems for family and peers who further motivated her to enhance her writing skills and develop her craft by taking poetry workshop classes at San Francisco City College. Trina desired to share her love of poetry to a broad audience. As a result, she entered poetry contests and was featured in numerous public performances throughout San Francisco. The Journey | Trina has her work published in books and featured in several newspapers. She is the author of a published book entitled, A Sister, A poet, A Spiritual Spoken Word (2013). In addition, her work has been featured in the following publications: ♦ Street Sheets (February 2017) ♦ Poor Magazine (March 2012 – February 2016) ♦ The San Francisco Guardian (March 2012) ♦ The SF Bay View (March 2012)

Author Trina Brigham is a native of San Francisco. She grew up in the Visitation Valley neighborhood located in San Francisco-- where she attended elementary and middle school. She graduated from Las Flores Continuation School in Sacramento, California.

A Sister, A Poet, A Spiritual spoken word is a collection of short stories arranged in a poetic context. It expresses the complexities of life from various personal perspectives concerning love, hope, and things to come.

Author Trina Brigham has used examples of her personal experiences to relate to readers as she embraces her experiences of life, love, and spirituality. This dynamic book searches the mind, body, spirit, and confronts fears and questions that most people never make evident to themselves or others. Trina exposes the inadequacies of our nature by speaking truth as the Holy Spirit bear witness and utterance to foretell the present and future. Under God's anointing insight by revelation God speaks to the hearts of the people through messages, instructions, and poetic content.

A sister, A Poet, A spiritual spoken word has been divided into three categories to give the reader a clear understanding of how each part of our well- being is essential to our growth and must be acknowledged and nurtured to grow as we complete the journey of life.

A Sister represents the physical women her weakness her strengths and vulnerability. The poet represents the inner man constantly searching as we pursue our journey in hopes to find his identity and purpose for life. A spiritual spoken word speaks volumes to its readers bearing as a witness to the holy spirit that words serve as a key factor to address the issues that gives us the power and authority to speak things into existence.

www.ingramcontent.com/pod-product-compliance
Lightning Source LLC
LaVergne TN
LVHW040157080526
838202LV00042B/3200